The 7 MIND SHIFTS

TO IGNITE YOUR SUCCESS

The 7 MIND SHIFTS
TO IGNITE YOUR SUCCESS

Claudia Cooley

Published by:
Claudia Cooley Inc.
Grand Terrace, CA 92313
www.ClaudiaCooley.com

Limits of Liability and Disclaimer of Warranty
The author and publisher shall not be liable for your misuse of this material. This book is strictly for informational and educational purposes.

Warning – Disclaimer
The purpose of this book is to educate and entertain. The author and/or publisher do not guarantee that anyone following these techniques, suggestions, tips, ideas, or strategies will become successful. The author and/or publisher shall have neither liability nor responsibility to anyone with respect to anyone with respect to any loss or damage caused, or alleged to be caused, directly or indirectly by the information contained in this book.

ISBN 978-0-9856026-1-1 paperback
Library of Congress Cataloging-in-Publishing Data is available upon request.

Printed in the United States of America. First Printing, 2015

Front Cover Design by Epiphany Marketing
www.EpiphanyMarketingFirm.com
Back Cover Design by Creative Linc Marketing
www.CreativeLinc.com
Interior Design by Creative Linc Marketing
Editing by Get Branded Press www.GetBrandedPress.com
Back Cover Photography by Raul Lozano

To my seven amazing joys of my life, my grandchildren, who inspire me to give my best back to the world... because they would never allow me to do less.

These are the bright stars that light up my horizon because I know there is greatness in each of them.

Acknowledgments

I am grateful for my Dad, who gave me my very first inspiration to become an Entrepreneur and to always have a heart for people. That legacy has served me well as I've been able to follow that path and to live a life that I love.

To my husband of over 50 years, I say thank you for all of your support and for celebrating every victory and win – whether big or small – with me. He makes my dreams possible.

Over the years I've had amazing mentors and this project was born from an idea inspired by one, Bob Donnell. Thank you.

Thank you to those in my corner who cheer me on, give me encouragement, and when needed, advice and technical support.

A special thank you to my creative team and their great collaborative efforts: Rasheed Louis and Epiphany Marketing for sharing your friendship, creative powers and IT expertise. Susie Augustin and Get Branded Press for lovingly editing, advising, and overseeing important aspects to complete the project on time. Amy Pulliam and Creative Linc Marketing for artistically creating the layout and other needed contributions.

I thank God for all of the opportunities that have come my way to do what I love to do, helping others to live their lives in balance and inspire them to reach for their dreams.

To my family, friends and cheerleaders that always believe in my possibilities, I'm grateful.

CONTENTS

INTRODUCTION

Ignite Your Success

Building your life on your own terms is a very exciting journey. The keys for designing a life that you love are found in creating balance in all areas of your life.

We call it "Success Synergy". Balance in your Health, Wealth, Relationships, and Goals that lead to a Legacy and how you show up for the world - Your Branding.

The 7 Mind Shifts coaching concepts give you every tool, inspiration and motivation *to IGNITE Your Success.*

Many of the golden nuggets you will experience are tried and true by hundreds of those I've had the opportunity to coach, teach and train over the years from the boardroom to the classroom. I can tell you as I've learned the value of not being in a Mindset, but allowing myself to have a Mind Shift, success in every area of my life excelled, and yours will too.

The ability to move forward powerfully to reach your dreams and your "Pot of Gold at the end of the Rainbow" exist when we embrace the REAL magic formula for success.

R • Realize your vision and purpose

E • Energize your abilities, talents and gifts

A • Accelerate your action steps

L • Live your life out loud, with fun and freedom

What area of your life are you trying to improve? With the 7 Core Strategies you will be building new muscles and new thinking to master the Mind Shifts to have the success story you desire in any or all areas of your life.

Many years ago, our son Ryann traveled to China with a college photography study group. Approximately 30 students scattered upon arrival and traveled to China's main attraction and touristy areas. Ryann, with his pilgrim's passion, headed for the less traveled regions that he had researched beforehand to determine where he would be able to capture his perfect picture. He really wanted this and just knew his *picture* awaited him at the top of a well-known mountain.

Beginning his long hike up the mountain, he was excited and couldn't wait to find this long awaited goal. By evening, as it began to get dark, he was only halfway up, and stumbled upon a monastery where he was greeted and welcomed to stay for the night. These warm and loving men were living in silence, so no conversation could have taken place to prepare him for what he would discover at the end of the next day.

As he continued his journey upward, he became more excited for the opportunity that lay ahead and this excitement drew him closer and closer to what he'd hoped for. Yes, his determination, commitment and desire to get to the top of his mountain, to get the best view and capture the best picture, propelled him to the top.

Pulling himself over the last ledge, trembling with excitement and exhaustion, he looked up to take in not only the beautiful view he'd hoped for, but was startled to see a bus blow past him. Wow, there was a road up here? He could have made this trip much easier, faster and in comfort?

What a profound lesson life had taught not only him but me, too. Immediately, I thought of how this lesson applies to my work as a professional and life enrichment coach. To get where we want to go faster – to reach our own Mountain Tops full of goals, visions and dreams – we need a road map, tools, appropriate expectations, and a nice ride for the journey.

Today, I spend most of my time helping men and women reach their Mountain Tops even faster, enjoy the ride and celebrate who they are becoming on the journey.

Join us for the 7 Core Strategies and opportunity to apply it to your life immediately using the included Action Guide.

Mind Shift 1

Mind Shift 1

Your Vision Empowered by Your Dream

*When you take your first step
it takes a vision empowered by your dreams
with the action to create a life in balance
as you rev up for real success.*

Today we are starting on a journey to create a Life in Balance that empowers your Health, Wealth and Relationships, for living an Extraordinary Life. These 7 *Mind Shifts* will identify the areas of life that must be considered to Rev Up for Success and live a life you love – a life that's fulfilling, and full of fun and freedom.

In *Living your Life in Balance*, we always consider the 5+1 Essential Elements: Health, Wealth, Relationships, Accomplished Goals, and Professional Image (Branding).

Where do you want to start? What area do you feel you are struggling with?

The 7 Mind Shifts will provide the information and ideas that will set you on a course of success like none other, in one or all of the areas that you have decided to work on, and you will have the tools to apply in the right away.

**Your Vision Empowered by Your Dream =
The Beginning of Your Journey to REAL Success**

Your Vision is the big picture of what's possible. Your Vision is simply seeing something that you can envision in your mind. Combining that with what you see, and believe you can achieve, gives your mind the ability to take quantum leaps into the "what if onlys" and on to even more "what is possible".

There are No Limits. Your *Dreams* are the "emotions" that fuel your Vision with:
- Aspirations
- Ambitions
- Energy

to accomplish bigger things!

The Vision is the Vehicle
The Dreams are the Gas

Your Dream is like a rubber band that pulls your vision into existence. Try to picture this in your mind. If you hold both index fingers up and wrap a rubber band around each of them or your hands, then start pulling each in the opposite direction, you will feel the tug for the other finger or hand to follow. Your Dreams are like this and will pull your vision into reality. So *Dream*, and *Dream Big* while you are at it.

Why is this so important to know? It can be the difference in being happy or living disappointed. Now, I'm sure you are wondering, "What if I don't know what my Vision is?" I will help you understand how to build a big, clear and powerful vision. Let's start here, using your imagination.

What do you want your life to be in the next 5-10 years?

1. In your relationships? In your health?

2. In your finances? (write a number down)

3. How would you like to earn that money - dream job or business? (lottery is a big gamble)

4. How do you envision yourself?

5. What kind of house do you live in?

6. What car are you driving?

7. How and where are you creating fun and freedom into your life?

8. Who are your friends?

9. Write down your answers whether you believe they are possible or not. We are creating your Vision.

Dreaming supports your belief and soon you will become engaged in the possibilities. Our dreams embrace our most cherished longings and identity.

"If you can DREAM it, you can ACHIEVE it."

~ Zig Ziglar ~

Not so long ago, I had a client that wanted help getting healthy, and at first I just couldn't determine how to motivate him to accomplish what he wanted. Then I asked him what health looked like to him, and had him write out a description. When he shared his Vision of Health, I asked if he could picture himself there. He couldn't quite do it, so I asked him, "Why do you want to be healthy? What do you dream of doing when you reach your goal?"

Now we got to the core. He really wanted to be healthy and energetic enough to play with his grandkids. They always wanted him to play hide and seek, and he had to stand at the tree because he couldn't run and hide. Now his emotions became evident and these emotions triggered his dream that he could see himself healthy and playing with his amazing grandkids.

Starting with this vision, he began to see it and the dream delivered the reality. About four months later he was running and having fun with those kids, all at a healthier weight. He even achieved more than he envisioned. He started buying smaller clothes and was really enjoying how he looked.

I've worked with people that have lost their dreams. They really felt as if they were on a downhill slope, slippery at that, and no way to stop. This mindset plays out harshly on Relationships, Health and certainly accomplishing the desired Wealth. Don't be discouraged, here are some easy things to do to stop the downward slide, and start to climb again.

Having a Big Dream is Essential

1. One of my Clients told me, "For years, I went through the motions until one day I realized that I was so caught up in day-to-day living that I forgot all about my Dream and my future goals. How did this happen? I stepped back and took some time to remember my original Dream and reason for doing what I was doing, and it all returned and refueled me and got me back on course. Today, my life is rich and fulfilled."

2. It requires focus to act on your Dream.

3. It takes a plan to make your Dream real.

4. Let others help you act on your Dream.

5. When working together for a common goal, I believe ordinary people can achieve extraordinary things.

"Feel the POWER that comes from focusing on what EXCITES you."

~ Oprah Winfrey ~

ACTION GUIDE

ACT ON YOUR DREAM! To achieve the future you want, you must identify with what you really want to do, get connected to the emotions of that dream, and then *act on it!* Start on it today. If you don't, in a year you will wish you had.

ASSIGNMENT 1

Begin your journey to outrageous success and live an integrated life with balance. These 6 easy-to-do steps will turn *Dreams* into reality.

1. Get in touch with your *Dreams*. Create a Dream/Vision Board. Cut out pictures of things you love (not just like) from magazines or on the Internet. These can include: food, travel, people,

homes/furnishings, clothing, jewelry, inspirational words, and indicators of your spiritual journey. Make sure every picture is meaningful to you, then carefully and artfully attach them to a corkboard or a large poster board. Sit back and look at your project. Take in what came from your most inner self. These are your *Dreams* that fuel your vision.

2. Read books and listen to audios to capture stories of people who have done what you want to do. See how they followed their own *Dreams* and take notes. What did they do that resonates with you? You'll know when you say, "I can do that."

3. Establish a community. Find others that will support your dreams. Have mentors and coaches that you admire that can help you empower your vision.

4. Identify possible obstacles that might stand in the way of your *Dreams*. Evaluate if they are important enough to sidetrack your path. It's always important to evaluate what's between your ears. Was a seed of failure or discouragement planted, or even an untruth that you believed that has become a roadblock to your success? Check out if your *Mindset* needs a *Mind Shift*.

5. Make necessary changes in your life to break the cycle that keeps you from moving forward or even keeps you frozen from stepping forward. Is it a fear of failure, a fear of rejection? I love to brush off my shoulder as if the "evil one" is sitting there to

discourage me. I say, "You aren't even real. You are just an illusion." Just this one action made a huge difference in my own growth.

6. Set clear, exciting and inspiring goals.

Have a Vision, A Dream and Believe

- ↗ Step into Action

- ↗ Dream a Big Dream

- ↗ And Enjoy your Endless Possibilities

Mind Shift 2

Mind Shift 2

Inspire Confidence and Belief in Yourself

*It's all about confidence and the belief in yourself
to reach your vision and dream.
To stretch for your A+ that is in you,
and to never ever settle for second best.*

Self-confidence is crucial and is a cornerstone of positive living. It affects how you think, act and even how you relate to others. It allows you to live your life to your full potential. Luckily, self-confidence is a seed already planted deep inside of you. You don't have to go in search of it, you just have to cultivate it, feed it and keep it nourished, and it will serve you well.

*"With CONFIDENCE,
you have WON before you have started."*

~ Marcus Garvey ~

So what is Self-Confidence? I like to put self-confidence and self-esteem together when creating a power tool for our success.

- ↗ Self-Confidence – a feeling of trust in one's abilities, qualities and judgment

- ↗ Self-Esteem – a healthy belief in oneself and respect for one's worth

I feel it's so important to talk about self-confidence, in believing in ourselves to become unstoppable. This is the next key to reaching our dreams and rev up our success. I believe we have the capacity to be successful in all areas of our life.

"As is our CONFIDENCE, so is our CAPACITY."

~ William Hazlitt ~

Health • Wealth • Relationships

What gets in our way? It's our mindset!

- ↗ We settle on what's safe or easy

- ↗ We have a fear of failure or a fear of rejection

- ↗ We don't believe we are good enough or have what it takes to be really successful

ACTIVITY 1

Write on a Post-it note "I'm more than enough."

Fill an entire Post-it note pad with those words and stick them everywhere in your home, including the bathroom mirror. Also, in a book you are reading, your car, handbag or briefcase. Everywhere in your range of sight.

We give ourselves a back door out when we say, "I've never been successful," "I'm not smart enough," "I don't need much, I don't mind settling," or "It's no big deal if I do well or not. No one really cares anyway."

**Negative Comments Are Like
Black Specks In White Paint**

We are all born into this world like buckets of white paint and by the time we are 21 years old our white paint starts to become grey because black specks are being dropped into our white paint. The black specks are negative comments that either we drop into our paint or others do.

You might say to yourself that you are stupid when you don't get an A on a paper or project. Other ways you might make negative comments is saying you aren't smart enough, pretty or handsome enough, clever enough, or even fast enough to get that job, promotion or new client.

Someone else may drop black specks into your paint and not even know it.

When our daughter was born we already had two sons and were totally ecstatic to finally have a girl. We hadn't planned her and would often, in love, call her our "surprise package". When she was nine, I overheard her telling one of her little friends that Mommy and Daddy didn't love her. We only loved her brothers because we had planned to have them. If only she knew the truth. But because we had called her our surprise, she discounted that we wanted her and cherished her. And this, my friend, was how we dropped black specks into her bucket of white paint.

My sister once told me I had lips like my oldest sister. This sister had always been overweight and I, at 12 years old, had just been put on my first doctor's diet. Now my assumption was that I was going to grow into the lips that represented being overweight. I practiced in front of a mirror for six months to hold my lips in a different way. I know how silly this sounds, but we all do it, all the time.

So how do we make the Mind Shift to a healthier mind and self-esteem? We put the lid on our bucket and protect it from any more black specks contaminating our white paint. When someone makes a comment, if it really isn't valuable, let it slide away. Say something positive to yourself in its place. We can talk ourselves into a higher level of self-confidence; we can even talk ourselves into a better mood. Words are powerful. Watch how you use yours and how you allow other's words to impact you.

ACTIVITY 2

Put the book down and get a clean sheet of paper. Divide it in half vertically by folding it down the middle and give it a soft crease. Open it back up. Now on the left side of the paper make a list of 25 of your greatest characteristics. On the right side, make a list of five negative characteristics about yourself. Only five.

When you finish, I know you will see you are pretty amazing. Now, just put this by the side of your bed and read it every night and every morning. You will start to love yourself and your life.

You know, building our confidence is really simple. It's knowing your value and purpose.

My Mind Shift Began Here In My Story

There is a lot of talk about Purpose in the world today, but I didn't always know I had a Purpose and wanted to leave a Legacy. I was so busy working and raising my kids, enjoying the day-to-day routine, that I didn't even give it a second thought until I was about 32 years old.

I had just started teaching Professional and Personal Image Development and decided to purchase a franchise with Image Improvement, Inc. The company owner, Joanne Wallace, was my mentor and I thought she was amazing! She always looked fabulous, presented herself perfectly, carried many titles in the industry, and was well-respected throughout America for her expertise. I wanted to be just like her, but there were a few problems with that.

First, she is really tall, and I'm only 5'2". Second, she was extremely self-confident, and because I didn't believe in my own abilities, I copied her carefully and utilized her methods instead of trusting my own instincts. Third, I dressed like her (since she knew more about professional dress than I did). Then I tried to teach like her. And then, well, you get the picture. This went on for almost a year before I had a life-changing vision.

My Vision of Heaven's Workshop

I found myself in a workshop of sorts. There was a worktable in the middle of the room, and there were dozens of cubbies attached to the wall and wrapped around the entire room. I wonder what's inside of those cubbies? Soon, little angelic creatures were flitting around the room and bringing items from the cubbies to the worktable. What are they doing? It didn't take me long to recognize some of the items: body parts like short and chubby legs, curly and thin hair, freckles and personality traits like compassion, a hot temper, a knack for learning, impatience, high-energy, and a need for control. Hmmm...why are those familiar?

The pile of items was growing, and I could hardly take my eyes off all of the activity. Eventually, I glanced to my side and gasped under my breath. Is that who I think it is? Standing at the other end of this long wall, I saw God in all of His glory. He was paying careful attention to the activity of the angels and what was happening on the worktable; His hand resting on his chin, deep in thought.

Somehow, I turned my eyes back to the worktable. The angels were assembling the items, and I couldn't wait to see what they were making. Then I saw what was taking shape on the table and understood why it was all so familiar. That's me! Look at the chubby thighs, the freckles, the hair. It's me! I was amazed at what I was seeing, and yet those particular features made me feel frustrated, the same way they did every time I looked in the mirror.

I quickly glanced back at God. He was smiling and nodding His head, and then He did this amazing thing. He spoke. "Yes. This is exactly what I had dreamed she would be like. She will be short and have to watch her weight. She will never reach a top cupboard, but I will give her a son to do that for her someday. She will be short-waisted, have a crooked nose and a hot temper, and be a bit of a perfectionist. I'm so pleased."

What? He's pleased? But I never liked my crooked nose, and I'm tired of the weight. Part of me was hoping those angels would fix those features for me, as they were still flitting around here and there. I was wishing and hoping until His voice interrupted my thoughts.

"Stop! Don't add or take away one more thing. She is perfect." He put His stamp of approval on me and said, "Ship her out. She is perfect for the mission I have for her. No one else but she will be able to do the job I've lined up for her to do. When she figures out how to shed the weight, she'll help others do it too. When she learns to take all of that high-energy and perfectionism and direct it toward living her Purpose, she'll inspire others to do the same."

I realized at that moment that waving my "magic wand," always wishing I looked or acted differently the way I had done for years, was not God's desire for me.

Every time I had looked in the mirror, every time I lost my temper, every time I saw someone I wanted to emulate, I would wave that magic wand and wish that I could look differently and act differently. I wish I didn't have a crooked nose, I wish my hair wasn't so curly, I wish I didn't always have to watch my weight, and on and on. But it was suddenly very clear that I wasn't supposed to look, dress, talk, or train like my mentor or anyone else. I was supposed to take what I was learning and do it my own unique way.

I now understood that He had uniquely designed me with my assets and deficiencies to accomplish a specific Purpose in this world. I could see that He had not only designed me, but that He had perfectly shaped my life experiences to prepare me for my Purpose. I didn't need to work on being like someone else. I just needed to work on being myself - the best self I can be to make a difference in someone else's life, to make a contribution to others.

So, the things I can change in my life, I work on. I've learned how to curb the hot temper and redirect my perfectionism. I've learned how to release the weight and keep it off. But the things I can't change, I have learned to celebrate. Will I ever be 5'7"? No. Do I really need to straighten my nose or get rid of the freckles? No, not really. So these I will celebrate.

This was a real turning point for me. I found new freedom and began to really grow into who I am. There is only one you and one me, and we each have a Purpose unique to us. We each need to reach for our own potential. This truly frees us to realize Passion and Power in our lives. That's why the license plate on my hot ride reads "Free To Be Me" (FRTOBME).

When you step into your uniquely designed Purpose, you will find your Passion...AND you will become powerful in making a difference in those around you and the world. It's true, and it is the richest discovery I have ever made.

You Will Find That When You Stop Waving Your Magic Wand, Your Passion Will Kick In

Now you know without a doubt you have real value, a real purpose so take your next steps:

- ➤ Energize your talents, abilities and gifts, finding ways to use them daily

- ➤ Celebrate your wins

You will automatically be more confident, because you know you don't have to be like anyone else, you are more than enough, and living your purpose will make your life "Juicy".

Mrs. Lowly and Mrs. Big

Mrs. Lowly goes to church and sees Mrs. Big standing by the door. "Wow, that woman has really got it all together," thinks Mrs. Lowly. "Just look at her grace. See how intelligent she is. She dresses nicely too. Boy, I didn't fix my hair right this morning; my dress doesn't look very nice and so I guess I'd better not even try to talk to her. I don't have anything to offer her, so I'll just slip out the other door." To be honest, I have to admit I've done this on occasion! So Mrs. Lowly goes out the back door because she doesn't feel "good enough" about herself to say anything to Mrs. Big. But Mrs. Big, who in her own mind sees herself as a "Mrs. Little", sees Mrs. Lowly leave. Mrs. Big is offended because she saw Mrs.

Lowly, whom she thinks of as a "Mrs. Large", snub her! "That lady doesn't like me," she thinks. And that's the way the game plays out. We hurt others and ourselves without even knowing it when we allow our own self-doubt to cloud our thinking.

"BELIEVE in yourself! Have FAITH in your abilities! Without a humble but reasonable confidence in your own POWERS you cannot be SUCCESSFUL or happy."

~ Norman Vincent Peale ~

ACTION GUIDE

DISCOVER YOUR PURPOSE

Purpose is usually a combination of what you love to do and what you are really good at. We don't come with those talents and gifts to leave them behind, and love doing things we aren't even passionate about. Some people discover their Purpose quickly, others need more time.

ASSIGNMENT 1

Finding your unique purpose may take some time and reflection, but I've included an exercise that may help you get there more quickly. Go ahead and give it your best shot.

1. Write down everything you love doing, everything you are really good at doing and everything you would really like to have in your life. On your sheet of paper, narrow your list down to five.

2. Ask yourself if there is a way for you to combine what's left on your list of what you love doing and what you want to have. Write all of the possibilities down.

ASSIGNMENT 2

Feed your Self-Confidence and Self-Esteem

1. Ask three people (friends, family or even business associates) to write down and give you in a sealed envelope, what your good qualities are, and your negative qualities. Don't be afraid. You will be surprised how this will build your confidence, and also give you constructive input in areas you can work on to grow into who you are becoming.

ASSIGNMENT 3

Renew your Self-Confidence and Self-Esteem Daily

1. Prepare for your journey; set your goals.

2. Set out on your journey; create measurable actions steps.

3. Accelerate towards success; know you can do it.

4. Celebrate your successes; start journaling daily.

> *"The act of taking the FIRST STEP*
> *is what separates the WINNERS from the losers."*
> ~ Brian Tracy ~

Mind Shift 3

Mind Shift 3

Determination + Commitment + Perseverance

It's time to add the polish and the fuel,
to give you the energy and stamina to play full out
and be ready to play your bigger game.
Remember, it's like you to do well.

One of my favorite movies is *Rudy*, an American inspirational sports film. I used to show it to my High School Marketing/Business classes every year when I was a teacher, to inspire my kids to never give up, to not listen to others' opinions of what their possibilities can be, and to do every potential thing to get prepared to accomplish their dreams.

There are other movies that deliver this message and do it well, and you might be more familiar with *The Rookie*, *Million Dollar Baby* or even *Chariots of Fire*. It doesn't matter which one you pick that inspires you, just watch it again. Then, go back and visit your Mind Shift 1 Assignment around your Vision and Your Dream.

Can't you already begin to feel more inspired to reach your dream when remembering the strong message of the movie you reflected on, and how it moved you at the time? Now apply that same emotion and energy to your Vision and you will become more than just determined to go full out to achieve it, you will stay in the game all the way to victory.

"The DIFFERENCE between
the impossible and the POSSIBLE
lies in a person's DETERMINATION."
~ Tommy Lasorda ~

Determination

Go to work and really discover the key elements of your vision, and the steps that need to take place to get where you are headed. You've already determined your destination. How do you get there and what can you do to ensure the journey is successful?

1. Develop an awareness of the process.

2. Stay focused.

3. Maintain a positive attitude, an "I can do it" attitude.

Read books that will give you tools and strategies to support your deepest desires to go after what you want:

↗ *Think and Grow Rich* by Napoleon Hill

↗ *One Great Goal* by Ursula Mentjes

↗ *The Four Agreements* by Don Miguel Ruiz

↗ *How Successful People Think* by John C. Maxwell

> *"Failure will never overtake me*
> *if my DETERMINATION to SUCCEED*
> *is strong enough."*
> ~ Og Mandino ~

Commitment

Commitment is the attitude of someone who works hard to do what they have promised to do.

Think of the commitment that is made when you fall in love and decide to build a life together. You share rings, promise to be faithful and love each other deeply forever. This is a commitment that my husband and I made over 50 years ago, and continue to benefit from the joyous outcome of that commitment. When you make a commitment to someone, even yourself, it has the implication of a guarantee attached. I can see the product tag dangling with the pledge of the promise identified right there in plain sight. This carries the same power when you make a commitment to yourself; guaranteeing you are going to do everything it takes to realize a great outcome on your success journey.

Your *Determination* is your conviction, your *Commitment* is your promise to work hard with dedication (it's your personal guarantee), and your *Perseverance* is the "I'll never quit" tenacity required to get all the way to the Gold.

I think of Job in the *Bible*. At first he was a very blessed man, being of great wealth, friendships and health. Then his world fell apart and he lost his health, friendships and wealth; all that was dear to him. But he never gave up; he still believed he was loved by God and never gave up hope. Then his life turned back around and everything was returned to him plus even more. Why? His belief.

A great story to remind us to jump in the game and stay in the game. That's where the rewards are. Another example is *Think and Grow Rich* by Napoleon Hill, where it describes the miner that dug for gold. He worked with real dedication as he was discovering small amounts of gold and was spurred on until the gold veins dwindled to almost nothing. Tired and without success, he finally gave up and let his mine return to the bank and he headed back home, leaving his dreams behind. Then when the mine was purchased and prospecting began again, they found the past miner had stop just short of his dream, three feet short of the biggest gold vein ever reported. When times get tough and you get discouraged, do you have the tendency to give up and settle for less than your dream? If you do, remember this story and leave no stone unturned until you find a solution, encouragement, support, new ideas and refreshed energy to continue on.

> *"WINNERS are ordinary people*
> *with extraordinary DETERMINATION."*
>
> ~ Unknown ~

Perseverance

Perseverance is the quality that allows someone to continue trying to do something even though it's difficult, there's opposition or even some failure. They pull from something deep inside, something planted there, their "Success Seed", to keep on keeping on.

John Maxwell encourages us to take the word "Quit" out of our dictionary, actually cut it out. There is a military saying that goes like this, "When the times get tough, the tough get going."

How tough are you? Can you hang tight when things look rough? What are you willing to do to insure that the bad times don't last long or that you can get right back up if you have some failures?

> *"PERSEVERANCE is the hard work you do*
> *after you get tired of doing the HARD WORK*
> *you already did."*
>
> ~ Newt Gingrich ~

Donald Trump definitely bounces back from failure. You know why; he knows he has the success tools in him, and he will go back and do what made him successful the first time. Again.

It's what he calls "thinking like a champion". How can you think like a champion? "I believe business is very much about problem solving. If you can learn to deal with and solve problems, you will have a much bigger margin for success." And that's his secret for bouncing back! This man has great self-confidence.

Fortunately, it's YOUR privilege to think like a champion and use these Success Seed Tools:

1. To FOCUS on the solution rather than the problem.

2. To THINK positively in the midst of negative circumstances.

3. To maintain an ATTITUDE of confidence and calmness in the midst of turbulent circumstances.

4. To Keep on WORKING toward a solution; instead of worrying, wishing and waiting.

There are times we'll experience "potholes in the road," and if the view isn't clear ahead, we might step into one. When I interview on my radio show *Rev Up For Success Radio*, I invite people that have been on their success journey, have learned some serious lessons along the way, and are willing to "pay it forward" by reaching back and helping others become successful, miss the potholes, and know how to maneuver around detours/roadblocks successfully.

**I believe we don't have to step into the potholes,
if we know where they are and what we're looking for.
As for roadblocks and detours, I feel these are the
opportunities to be creative and explore something
new and see what we've never seen before.
It's an adventure.**

However, I recently did just that, one night on my way to speak to a Women's Group. The parking lot was dark, I wasn't familiar with the location, and when I turned from clicking my key to lock my car, I stepped sideways into a fairly deep pothole. I lost my balance; pitching things I was holding to free my hands to cushion the fall.

This all happened so quickly that I found myself laying on the ground in the dark, and no one was around. Now of course you know our normal reaction; hop up, dust yourself off and see if anyone saw you make a fool of yourself. Then you check for broken bones or sprained ankles. And I was most concerned if I'd torn the knee in my pants, since I still needed to go in front of an audience and speak.

I survived the pothole that night with just a few scrapes, and being fully committed to my mission, I climbed the stairs and marched right in to the event without disclosing any evidence of my mishap. I believe I was able to deliver an inspiring talk in spite of the jar to my body and ego; went home and the next day experienced some of the ramifications of stepping into a pothole.

But I must say, I find this a great opportunity to share with you that it isn't any fun hitting the potholes, so avoid them at all costs if possible.

Listen to those that give good advice, soak it up, and learn from the mistakes of others. Just like our parents told us, "Do as I say, not as I do." So our mentors might say, "Learn from what I did, listen to my better choices."

Find mentors, read books, go to seminars and hang out with people that are determined, committed and persevere.

ACTION GUIDE

ASSIGNMENT 1

Watch this YouTube Video (9:35 powerful minutes). *A must-do assignment, please don't skip.*

The Best Determination Ever
Amy Purdy - Living Beyond:
https://www.youtube.com/watch?v=yiKGbHxzMgg

ASSIGNMENT 2

Using a problem you might be facing at the moment, or in the past, work it through the Success Seed Tools to come up with a solution. If you can't think of one, use your imagination.

ASSIGNMENT 3

Most business owners have experienced difficult times, periods when your finances were lean or business performance didn't quite meet your expectations. But when a business is teetering on the brink of failure, you have two choices: You can throw in the towel or persevere despite the odds.

Take a look at eight entrepreneurs who could've given up, but instead chose to look failure in the eyes and fight their way back. You will find one that you can relate to or be encouraged and inspired by.

- Donald Trump

- Martha Stewart

- Ben Cohen & Jerry Greenfield / Ben & Jerry's Ice Cream

- Harland "Colonel" Sanders / KFC

- Gary Heavin / Women's World of Fitness Club

- Steve Jobs / Apple

- Howard Schultz

Mind Shift 4

Mind Shift 4

Enthusiasm Infuses Living a Life in Balance

Build your life by design.
Yes you can have it all.
You can create a life of abundance in your
health, wealth and relationships
for living a fulfilling, fun and prosperous life.
It starts here.

It's important to know that people notice us, build their first impression and even determine if they want to have a real relationship or do business with us within the first eight seconds of meeting.

Our First Impression is Created with Our Personality/Non-Verbal Language/Image & Appearance

CAREER AND LIFE DYNAMICS IN BALANCE

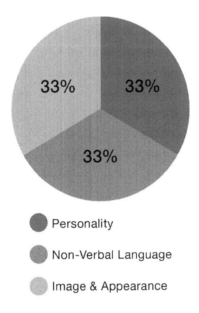

- ● Personality
- ● Non-Verbal Language
- ● Image & Appearance

Enthusiasm Infuses Our Personality

First, let's discover what enthusiasm is. Enthusiasm is the yeast that allows your excitement to rise to the surface and overflow to others. It's your zeal and passion for life. Enthusiasm is an outward expression of your emotions, energy and joy for what is happening and for the possibilities that are ahead. People gravitate naturally to enthusiastic people.

Have you ever gone to a party where you've arrived a bit late? When you got there you could tell there's something pretty cool going on within a group of people that continues to blossom into an even bigger group. What is so interesting that is causing the energy of this group to spread to even more people? Of course, you are curious and become anxious to join the group yourself. You ask, "What is the cause or source of this excitement?" It's like a magnet. The answer, "It's the enthusiasm of the young women sharing a story." There's that word again. Enthusiasm. This is something worth pursuing in your own life and personal growth.

You create significant relationships
with a magnetic personality.
If enthusiasm infuses our personality,
then a positive attitude feeds enthusiasm.

A positive attitude can be defined as a state of mind or a feeling based on beliefs, values and an attitude that shows up as optimism or optimistic. It's the old adage of the cup half empty or the cup half full mindset. I'm sure you've met people with each cup. I've recently discovered, it's not so important about how full your cup is, as long as you are open to others pouring into your cup to the full state. I, however, have known people that are even a cup overflowing.

1. My Dad embraced life, enjoyed it and lived full out.

2. My father-in-law was probably one of the most optimistic people I ever met and even up to his death at 98 years old, he still answered the phone every morning with a cheery "Gooood Morning" and you could just hear the intention for this to be a great day. Can't you just feel it?

3. Kim Somers Egelsee, a dear friend of mine and the author of the bestseller *Getting Your Life to a 10 Plus,* helps us discover how to experience life at the highest levels and to believe you can do it.

Enthusiasm is Energized When You Say YES

There is REAL power and energy that feeds your enthusiasm when you say "yes" to things that are aligned with your purpose. It's about saying "yes" to possibilities. Being ready to embrace the great opportunities that come your way and not letting them slip through your fingers or be looking the other way when "opportunity comes knocking".

This has been proven over and over in my life. When I was asked to become a franchise owner in Image Improvement, Inc., I ran from the opportunity for six months before I said "yes" and almost missed a life-changing event in my own possibilities. When I was asked to write a book for men, my first instinct was to turn and run, then remembered the power of "saying yes" and quickly let the word "yes" slip from my lips; then walked away scratching my head wondering what I'd really said "yes" to. However, things quickly began to miraculously align, including the title for the book that just showed up magically one morning.

Leaning into Opportunity

A few weeks later my next life lesson appeared. We were on our way to NYC for Christmas with our children, and as we were settling into our seats on the plane, the next opportunity arrived. Knowing that I needed to interview men from different industries to discover what the expectations were for being successful, I shouldn't have been surprised when a man that looked and dressed professionally took the aisle seat next to my husband. The door of the plane hadn't even closed, when I felt a nudge to lean across my husband to speak to this man. I said, "Hi, I happened to notice that you are dressed professionally, and by the way I'm writing a book for men called *From Dud to Stud... Revving Up for Success*. It's focused on professional and personal growth and wondered if you would be interested in being interviewed. He was really excited and leaned across my husband to tell me he loved this topic and not only attended seminars on the subject, but continually had trainings for his staff. Then the flight attendant tapped him and explained he was in the wrong seat and he had to move; but not before I gave him my card at his request.

By the time we had reached NYC, I checked my emails and he had already contacted me and wanted to know if I was serious, and did I want to meet face to face or by the phone. Immediately I returned the email stating face to face for sure. After sending the email, I scrolled to the bottom of the page and discovered he was V.P. of Deutsche Bank on Wall Street. That was where I held my first of the twelve interviews, at an amazing restaurant right on Wall Street. If I hadn't leaned forward into that opportunity on the plane, my life would be different, my opportunities for my future would be different, my influence in the world would be different. It's about leaning into opportunity, grabbing it and holding on tight.

Positive Attitude Begins with Positive Words

In the second Mind Shift we talked about the "Bucket of White Paint", stopping the negative self-talk, and even remembering to stop splattering black specks in others' buckets of white paint. Our self-talk is so powerful and if we change what we say, we can grow so much faster. Let me give you an example. Instead of saying you are so busy or too busy, change that and say, "I'm in demand".

How We See Ourselves and Others

We must first allow ourselves to be empowered by believing that we are designed with great gifts, talents and abilities like no one else. Next is to believe the same holds true for others that are in your life.

- ↗ You have everything you need in you already to be successful in reaching your vision and dreams
- ↗ Stop putting yourself down; forgive yourself for past mistakes
- ↗ Forgive others
- ↗ Appreciate others and their talents and abilities at work and home
- ↗ Send appreciation cards; say "thank you" often: receive compliments yourself!

I believe it is vital to celebrate who you are and empower others to do the same. In fact, my license plate reads "Free2BMe" because my journey is to help you be all you are meant to be, and ask that you help me be all I'm meant to be, too.

Enthusiasm Infuses Our Body Language & Conversation

1. Your Posture/Non-Verbal Communication. Do you have good eye contact, stand tall, have a great handshake, lean into a conversation? If you do, then great.

2. Your Facial Expressions. Do people ever say to you, "I thought you were such a snob when I first met you, but now that I know you, you are really nice."? Check yourself out next time when you're on a phone call by putting a mirror in front of you and see what your expressions are. Inviting? Friendly? Confident?

3. Verbal Communication. Speak up; use positive language, this will show confidence. Show a REAL interest in others by asking great questions and being a great LISTENER. Go online and research good conversation igniters. Carry them on a 3x5 card in your bag or pocket until you have learned them well.

"ENTHUSIASM is the yeast that makes your hopes SHINE to the stars. Enthusiasm is the SPARKLE in your eyes, the swing in your gait. The grip of your hand, the irresistible surge of will and the ENERGY to execute your ideas."
~ Henry Ford ~

Enthusiasm Infuses Our Outer Appearance

When we know we look our best our self-confidence goes up; we don't focus on ourselves but others. It's like the icing on the cake. We have a great personality, however if we let our outer image hold us back, people might miss us; unfortunately we are just a bit too much of a diamond in the rough.

Here are a few tools. Men, you can check my book *From Dud to Stud…Revving Up for Success* on creating the right branding for you. Ladies, my website will direct you to many of my workshops and resources to gain the insight you need to create your style.

1. Identify your image style.

   - What really catches your eye?

   - What are the professionals and successful people in your field wearing?

   - What's your lifestyle? Do you teach yoga, nurse injured animals back to health, change tires, or work in a corporate environment?

   - When you leave your house, what are you comfortable in? (But not sloppy or like you just fell out of bed.)

   - When you look in the mirror, does the image you see match your personality style and your business goals?

   - Above all, be authentic.

2. Use fresh and up-to-date dressing styles; know the trends, not fads.

3. Do your homework. Study TV actors and TV shows that represent your industry that are top drawer; i.e., News Commentators for those of you that are in the world of business; *The Good Wife*, *Suits*, and *Blue Bloods* for starters.

4. Be super spiffed up, clean and pressed, take it up a notch, check yourself out in a mirror before you leave home, and don't forget your hands. Check your nails (clean and short).

5. Ladies, accessorize but remember: more isn't always better. Take a count, if you have more than 20 different items, including buttons, glasses, patterns, jewelry, even accent detail on clothing, then you have crossed over…to entertaining.

6. Fellows, a quick tip – notice if your tie is the right width to work with the collar width of the shirt you are wearing, and then the lapel on your jacket. You just can't wear a 10-year-old shirt with a new tie or vice versa. It doesn't work. Polished shoes are always a must.

7. Dress for the level you want to reach in your success journey.

8. Keep breath mints with you.

9. Always reflect the very best of your inner self. Be authentic!

"LIVE YOUR TRUTH.
Express your love. Share your enthusiasm.
Take action towards your dreams. Walk your talk.
Dance and sing to your music. Embrace your blessings.
Make today worth remembering."
~ Steve Maraboli ~

ACTION GUIDE

BUILDING YOUR LIFE BY DESIGN

ASSIGNMENT 1

Email info@claudiacooley.com and request the following:

- ↗ *Top Ten Mistakes Women Make when Dressing Professionally*

- ↗ *Men's Top 10 Most Common Mistakes in Professional Dress*

ASSIGNMENT 2

Purchase Note Cards to have on hand.

1. Each night at the end of your day, write a few thank you cards to someone that you met in your day. Have the notes addressed and stamped, ready for mailing the next morning as you leave for your day.

2. Send appreciation notes and thank you notes to at least 10 people this week.

3. Stop reading and make the list right now.

ASSIGNMENT 3

Research at least five conversation-starter questions that you can use to connect with people on a higher level than just gathering business cards.

Mind Shift 5

Mind Shift 5

Significant Actions for Significant Outcomes

*Inspired confidence and belief in yourself.
Move forward with a plan and action steps.
These are the tools that move your wishes and dreams to a
reality. They will support you in playing a bigger game,
in showing up powerfully. Remember:
"How you do one thing is how you do everything."*

What is it that you want to achieve? Do you want to run a 10K Marathon, create a healthier weight, make more money, create more time with your family, take a great trip? What is it that resonates high on your list and mind right now? We know the best place to start is planning and preparation, then the action steps.

"ACTION is the foundational key to all SUCCESS."
~ Pablo Picasso ~

Live a Significant Life and Enjoy a Successful Business

In planning, we need to create a system that allows us to keep our lives in balance while accomplishing the things that move us toward our biggest goals. I love using jars filled with different sized rocks and sand to illustrate the pre-planning and planning to accomplish and have it all. You simply fill a jar with the different size rocks. Depending on how you fill it will affect how much you are able to do, and how much time you have left.

Start with the Big Rocks first; the most important life enriching and business effective goals and activities.

Why?

If you reverse the order, the jar fills with smaller rocks and sand first and then begins to overflow leaving the important things just sitting there ready to fall off. This means they may not happen at all.

The **Big Rocks** represent vacations, conferences and conventions that enhance the growth of your business or personal life, big projects like writing a book or memoir, creating a new business, weekend getaways, and time with the kids.

The **Medium Rocks** represent: staff meetings, business building activities i.e., networking, staff meetings, or even date night with your family.

Next, you will add small rocks and eventually the sand.

The **Small Rocks** represent: day-to-day tasks that keep the operation for your business or life running smoothly. A regular time to renew your spirit; include your hobbies, call back/follow up calls for your business, sending those thank you notes we talked about. Small rocks would also include going to the gym or creating an opportunity for movement or exercise; eating healthy daily and drinking lots of water, at least half of your body weight.

The **Sand** represents: checking email, going through mail, filing and keeping a clear space to work, calling some friends and social connection. It's all very important and needs to be included. This system will expand your possibilities of getting it all in your year.

When you do it the other way (the jar on the right), there is even room for more; more fun and more freedom.

Following this system or plan of putting the big rocks in first will allow you to accomplish even more, eliminate stress and enjoy the things that are important for you to live a life you love.

You can create your visual map by using a 12-month calendar; one of the most effective tools for creating a year and many years of significant accomplishments.

STEP 1: 12-Month "Big Rock" Calendar - Find the details in the Action Guide

STEP 2: Plan/Preparation

STEP 3: Strategic & Measurable Action

> *"Remember, a REAL DECISION is measured by the fact that you've taken NEW ACTION. If there's no action, you haven't truly decided."*
> ~ Anthony Robbins ~

ACTION GUIDE

We've all had moments when the light bulb came on, a great idea surfaces, or opportunity came our way.

That's when the implementation needs to happen for results to be realized. Insuring that procrastination, fear, anxiety or even stress don't become a roadblock and rob you of your dream and a great outcome. We must put powerful action steps in place.

Your Action Steps must be:

➢ Tangible

➢ Real

➢ Measureable

➢ Meaningful

➢ Doable

So let's get started.

The 3 Keys to Significant Outcomes & Accelerating Your Action

1. Be specific about what you want to achieve.

   - This is the most momentous piece; this has to come from your heart and deep inside

   - If it is meaningful and you own it, you can achieve it

2. Break through any barriers, roadblocks or mindsets to become unstoppable.

   - Determine what you truly believe you should focus on

- Does it *Rev You Up?*
- Expand your conversation to life-changing words
- Use 3x5 cards to write your words and inspiration that will motivate
- Imagine your possibilities
- Set positive intentions with accountability strategy
- Plug into others that will hold you accountable and believe in your possibilities strongly
- Take steps for Inspired Action
- Create action that inspires you and make it fun whenever possible; being successful doesn't have to be boring

3. Strategize your System for Success.

  a. Plan + Action = Results (predetermined actions to have a winning score).

  b. Create a Time Management system unique for you.

  - Make a list of steps – be clear about what you want to achieve
  - Create a time block 3+ times a week (power hour) to accelerate your progress
  - Create a space/environment that allows you to be efficient, focused, and mindful of what you are up to

  c. Create Accountability by using the Success Momentum Chart included on your ACTION GUIDE (with details how to use).

d. Additional Power Tools:

- Set up your calendar and color code by: activities, hats you wear, task and personal time
- Keep in Balance; Personally and Professionally
- Tell others what you are up to
- Ask someone to hold you accountable; this is why a coach is so helpful
- Have mentors that inspire you to stay motivated
- Create Focus

First, have your goals next to your bed and read before going to sleep and upon waking - YOU will become your own best accountability partner.

Second, use the Focus Cycle:

- Plan
- Act
- Evaluate/Reassess
- Enjoy Results
- Set next Stretch Goal and continue with this success cycle
- Now reward yourself – have some fun and see your next step as you enjoy your freedom in success

"The journey of a thousand miles begins with one step."
~ Lao Tzu (Low Taa) ~

ACTION GUIDE

ASSIGNMENT 1

Determine your One Great Goal for the year and complete the chart below by filling in the measurable action steps on the left and the date for completion on the left. Post this close to your work area and check it daily to make sure you are on course.

If course correction is needed, make the adjustment; however, I want you assess why you need the correction. If the needs or resources have changed that is one thing. But if you got off course, go to your accountability person and let them know to hold you to a finer line. Don't give into allowing excuses to get in the way, this could set you off course or close your doors quicker than stepping into quicksand.

DESIRED SUCCESS OUTCOME

Momentum
Action Steps

Measureable
Timeline

Current Reality

Date:

You will want to add many more lines to your chart and make several copies. This allows you to create one for the year, month and week, for any activity, goal or event you are involved in.

ASSIGNMENT 2

Purchase a 12-month calendar at a local stationery store or create your own by purchasing a small desk calendar that has 12 months. Tear it apart and attach it to poster board. Either way, fill in the Big Rocks first throughout the year with one color, and then add in the small rocks. Gravel and sand will take care of themselves; you don't have to plan for them with such dedication. However, they will still need to be accomplished, probably on your day planner. I color code my day planner, too: a different color for each of my businesses, a color for networking, a color for coaching and my favorite color for personal.

Mind Shift 6

Mind Shift 6

Build Your Community, Your Leadership and Your Tribe

Access the power of including others on the journey.
It's about the power of linking arms with others.
Building your community, your leadership and tribe
requires cultivating mentors, teams and leaders.
These are key areas to never neglect.

I call mentors "Balcony People." I shared about the importance of having the cheerleaders, coaches, and mentors in your life. It's too hard to go it alone and is a much slower journey. These are the people who see that success seed in you, when you can't.

MENTORS

"If you are the smartest one in the group,
you need some new friends."
~ Joel Osteen ~

- It's important to seek out someone who is at least 2 steps ahead of you to mentor you, someone you can be accountable to and someone you have respect for

- Look at areas of your life you want to develop or become stronger in; then find Master Mind Groups, Service Clubs, Rotary, Kiwanis, Trade Association groups

- Watch for the leaders and stay close to them to learn

- Attend seminars, workshops, and networking groups that inspire you and support you in moving to your next level

- Read and listen to "the Greats" in your field of interest for motivation and inspiration

- Find someone to be accountable to

- AND be a Mentor

"You are the average of the five people
you spend the most time with."
~ Jim Rohn ~

TEAMS

Teams are next in Building Community. Over a lifetime I've had many experiences in the area of building teams:

- One of my most successful and fulfilling is being married for over 50 years to a wonderful man
- Raising a family of 3 children and now 7 grandchildren
- Being a High School Teacher for over 20 years
- AND owning my own businesses

I found in being part of a team that the key ingredients are: The "I", the "We", and the "Team". The I and the We make a Team.

To empower our Team for success is to simply understand that we are all different; and how we can create success as we knit our differences together. (Grandma – Knitting uses 2 needles)

The Benefit for us is:

- Better relationships
- Financial success
- Personal success
- Bringing value to the lives of others through what we offer
- Contributing to others and the world

"If you help other people get what they want,
they'll help you get what you want."

~ Zig Ziglar ~

This happens when we:

⤷ Understand and utilize the differences and compliments of different leadership and behavioral styles

⤷ Learn to see, appreciate and respect the difference in others

Teamwork, teambuilding, and team effort all start with communication, which turns into conversation.

The 4 Key Conversation Tips

⤷ Draw on your own life experiences to set the stage to connect with another

⤷ Have great eye contact; be present in the conversation

⤷ Listen and HEAR – Be Focused; you are zeroing in on their feelings

⤷ Then feedback what you heard in your own words, and even add some of why it resonates with you, from your own life experience

EXAMPLE:
"You said '.....' and it makes me think of when I had a similar experience" (Don't one-up them, though.) "Is it like '.....'?"

It's like knitting two ideas together to create something even richer than the stand-alone concept. Or think of a dance, like a waltz, moving to the same music together, smoothly.

The final key in Building Community and your Tribe is in the area of being a Leader and Leadership.

LEADERS

It doesn't matter whether you are an entrepreneur, an executive, a manager and/or employee; improving your ability to lead others will change your results. Also, inspiring and encouraging others on your team to become leaders is a huge benefit to everyone. A truly "win-win" outcome.

KEY #1

Building Leaders within your sphere of influence.

When I was a teacher, I felt it was important to build leadership in each of my classes. I was trained to understand and use Emotional Intelligence to reach multiple learning styles and work successfully with various personality types. The next step was the most exciting, helping and supporting the discovery of each of the students' styles and building powerful teams by mixing the styles with balance. Can you just imagine how much you can accomplish in your company, family or even a team of volunteers if you use these simple tools? If my students' grades and camaraderie elevated from using this practice and system, think what you can achieve.

KEY #2

Being a leader, a true leader, you will lead from the back.

Lead by example, pave a clear path to follow, influence and empower them to do well, inspire them to use your example and with guidance tweak to fit their style, build their confidence by being a cheerleader and an encourager, then get out of their way.

KEY #3

Empower others by giving them the opportunity to work from their dreams and purpose.

It's so powerful to build relationships in business and personally when we honor the authenticity of another's dreams.

**Respect • Value • Appreciate • Honor
Let's talk about the four Leadership Styles.**

After years of researching, studying, practicing and teaching personality and behavioral styles, I knew it was essential to share this powerful information in a simple way. Using the Myers-Briggs system and the

DISC Behavioral Styles Assessments as a guide, I playfully transformed this amazing information into a fun and memorable game.

Over the years I have taught these ideas from the classroom to the boardroom and back again to hundreds of people, and on occasion when I bump into one of them, they'll let me know they married a Lion, or they are working with a Monkey. This tickles me that the information is memorable and useful. It makes improving your leadership FUN!

Lion • Monkey • Turtle • Giraffe
Four animals we'll use to discuss Leadership Styles.

See, after hearing those names you are already starting to make some assumptions about which animal exhibits certain characteristics. The diagram I've included in the Action Guide section will provide a visual picture of the two main characteristics:

- ↗ Assertiveness
- ↗ Responsive/Sensitivity

If you follow the numbers across the top of the diagram (Horizontal 1-10: The 10 indicates "most assertive".), you will see that the Giraffe is less assertive than the Lion, and the Turtle is less assertive than the Monkey. If you follow the numbers down the page on the left (Vertical 1-10: The 10 indicates "most responsive/ sensitive."), you will see that the Giraffe is less responsive/sensitive than the Turtle, and the Lion is less responsive/sensitive than the Monkey.

Before we go any further, I want to make it very clear. Each and every style is perfect. Remember, we are all designed with our own unique Purpose, Temperament and Gifts. This is simply a way to help you identify and maximize your leadership style and the styles of those you work with to achieve the best results and outcomes from working and personal relationships.

As a Lion/Monkey married to a Turtle, I can't tell you what a relief it was to step into our own style and not have to be status quo. My husband was taught he needed to be a Lion and he was exhausted trying to become something he wasn't. In my case, I was encouraged to be a Turtle, and if you ever meet me, you will know that was hard work and really impossible. What freedom we found in our own marriage when we played in the role we were designed for, and together we make a magnificent team.

Leadership Styles

1. Lion, Monkey, Turtle and Giraffe.

2. Characteristics of each one – In Action Guide.

3. Each one is "perfect", because this is how we are created.

4. Discover which ones are "You".

5. How to work with each of the styles that are different than your own style.

For the link to the video training on the Leadership Styles, email: info@claudiacooley.com
or visit: www.claudiacooley.com

Apply these strategies to your:
   a. Business
   b. Management position
   c. Working with others
   d. Building strong relationships at work/family

Building Your Tribe
When you share your vision with others and allow them to blend their dreams with your vision, you are going to see amazing things happen. This becomes your Tribe and this gives energy to your dream and theirs too.

**Have a VISION that motivates you and others
to achieve your desired life VISION.
Then do the same for them.**

I challenge you to be open and aware of those that are different than you, which is everyone, and create the space to work well together, learn from each other and build something strong for all of you.

ACTION GUIDE

ASSIGNMENT 1

Make a list of people you can support today. Recognize their dream.

ASSIGNMENT 2

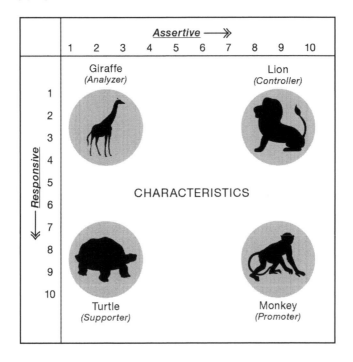

Discover Leadership Styles and the application for the everyday work environments and relationships.

   1. **Lion – Likes to Win**
- Controller
- Bottom line

- Delegates
- Time conscious
- Task oriented

2. **Monkey – Likes to be Recognized**
   - Promoter
   - Loves people
   - Enjoys life with a flair
   - Full of energy
   - Initiates team work
   - Creative

3. **Turtle – Likes to be Comfortable**
   - Supporter
   - Works well alone
   - Not a clock watcher
   - Loyal friend and employee
   - Works well with directions
   - Slow decision maker

4. **Giraffe – Likes to be Accurate**
   - Analyzer
   - Organized
   - Works alone well
   - Detail oriented
   - Thinks of the pros & cons
   - Excellent problem solver

What's YOUR Leadership Style?

"Coming together is a beginning.
Keeping together is progress. Working together is success."

~ Henry Ford ~

Mind Shift 7

Mind Shift 7

Have an Attitude of Gratitude & Contribution

*Living with an attitude of gratitude
that overflows into contribution
will make a difference in the world today.*

Gratitude is the final shift and the kick off to where real success begins! This is a really important consideration, it is the outcome of the other 6 sessions and the source for your future success, happiness and significance. You are now ready to build a powerful future, to make a difference in the world, your world, and creating the constant flow of abundance and possibilities. Creating an Attitude of Gratitude is a journey.

This has been my journey, a spiritual journey really, living life to accomplish my purpose, no matter what, through all circumstances. And now at this time of my life, I wake up each day full of Gratitude and a desire to live in Contribution, to make a difference in the world today. I wake up with my teeth chattering, I can't wait to see what the day brings. I'm READY, I'm EXCITED.

"We make a LIVING by what we get;
We make a LIFE by what we give."
~ Winston Churchill ~

How does the power of gratitude work?

Practicing gratitude involves being thankful for the little things, seeing all that happens in your life as a "miracle", and always being aware of the abundance in your life. There is always an immediate result: better relationships, better health, a more fun career journey, more happiness, and an overall increased quality of life. What is the secret to maximizing gratitude? First, try my formula. Start a Gratitude Journal.

Gratitude Journal

Buy a small spiral notebook and clip a pen to the spiral. Start with today, and put the date at the top of the page. Each day gets its own page even if you don't write something on it.

What I'm grateful for:

God	Family	Freedom	Mentors
Belief	Friends	Home	Abilities
Love	Health	Food	Tapestry
Husband	Energy	Knowledge	Balcony People

Gratitude Rock

Find a rock that feels good in your hand. Name it and carry it with you, along with your keys and wallet, or purse. When you touch it, it will remind you to say, "Thank you". You are learning to live your life as if everything were a miracle, and being aware on a continuous basis of how much you've been given. Gratitude shifts your focus from what your life lacks to the abundance that is already present.

The Benefit

Giving thanks makes people happier and more resilient, it strengthens relationships, it improves health, and it reduces stress.

> *"Gratitude makes sense of our past, brings peace for today, and creates a vision for tomorrow."*
> ~ Melody Beattie ~

Significance is in Contribution – Remember, you can't outgive.

Tapestry of Life

I love sharing about the Tapestry of our Life. It is the bridge between gratitude and contribution, the visual evidence of our life, becoming our best version of ourselves, and where we go from here; we become part of the tapestries of others.

My tapestry has evolved into the richest of colors as other lives have been woven into mine. I've watched my tapestry evolve from pastel colors from when I was younger into the deep, vibrant alive colors of today. This comes from having deeper value and contribution of relationships over the years.

What's really exciting is when we look at the underside of this artistic piece of fabric, you will find that there are broken threads and knots where new threads have been tied and woven in. My life tapestry just gets better, better, and so will yours.

Immediately use these Three Keys for *Revving Up Your Success*, creating great prosperity and living a happy fulfilling life.

"Success is KNOWING your purpose in life,
GROWING to reach your maximum potential,
and SOWING seeds that benefit others."

~ John Maxwell ~

You've heard the statement, "If you don't use it, you'll lose it"? Starting every day in gratitude starts the overflow to contribute to others, and this can be powerful for you and the recipient.

A while back John C. Maxwell spoke on the Success Magazine CD, regarding the difference between Success and Significance. Success is when you set goals and set out to achieve them with great outcomes. Significance is making a difference in someone's life, adding value to who they are and can become.

I'm determined to do that very thing; my desire is to become successful at becoming significant. I don't believe you can have true success without significance. Success is usually the steppingstone to significance.

There has to be a certain amount of success in people's lives before they are willing to take the step to significance, where they ask themselves, "What else is there in life beyond professional and monetary success?"

> *"Do all the good you can,*
> *by all the means you can,*
> *in all the ways you can,*
> *in all the places you can,*
> *at all the times you can,*
> *to all the people you can."*
> ~ John Wesley ~

It won't take you long when you look about yourself to observe what needs you see, and seize the moment to fill them. In the last few years I've heard of amazing things people are doing in other countries.

A woman I met from San Diego is helping young women in third world countries become entrepreneurs by using the jewelry they have so creatively made from paper, and are setting up businesses to provide for their families and communities.

Our Grandson has been involved in the past with an organization that supplies little chicks to depressed countries to teach them how to raise their own food and sell some to improve their economic state.

These are huge audacious goals, and I want to be making that kind of difference in the world too. Do you? We can. Remember, you can't outgive; what you give out comes back to you a hundredfold, so let's make it goodness.

"Help others achieve their DREAMS
and you will achieve yours."

~ Les Brown ~

On my radio show, *Revving Up For Success,* I interview people that are on their success journeys who are willing to "pay it forward", by reaching back and helping others coming up behind, to be successful on their journeys by missing the potholes and maneuvering the detours to reach their destination successfully.

Our most important question every day needs to be, "How can I make a difference in someone's life today, a smile, generosity, service?" What is the mission statement for your life? Out of that you will find the tools to live in contribution; being successful at being significant through your own purpose, heart and passion. Are you living your life of significance?

"To LOVE what you do and feel that it matters –
how could anything be more FUN?"

~ Katherine Graham ~

Live your extraordinary life with fun and freedom! Remember this isn't the end but just the beginning.

What is your "Pot of Gold at the end of the Rainbow?" Happiness?

Then step up and grab onto the life you really want.

ACTION GUIDE

ASSIGNMENT 1

Moving forward to your next step. Each session you have received new words to incorporate into your life strategically. And even though we have come to the end of *The 7 Mind Shifts to Ignite Your Success*, I feel compelled to leave you with one more word to ponder.

Use Your Next Word Often – ENDURANCE

- ➚ Build Your Endurance Muscle

- ➚ Enlist Your Courage

- ➚ Use Your Abilities

- ➚ Practice, Persistence, Tolerance

- ➚ Engage Your Stamina, Strength & Vitality

- ➚ Endurance is Your "Staying Power"

- ➚ Go for Your A+

- ➚ And Never, Ever Settle For Second Best!

Every Successful Person in Business or Even Sports Has a Coach or Mentor

If you don't, I invite you to join a group program, a 1:1 VIP program, or Mastermind programs at *Mind Shifts for Success Coaching to Rev Up Your Success.*

Every week we hold an online get together where I spend 30 minutes talking to you about your *Mind Shifts for Real Success* in every area of your life.

Create a life of balance and fulfillment, to achieve amazing results and outcomes.

Join the membership today. Provides lasting value and benefits you'll experience right away for you, your business and your family.

To join, visit:
www.claudiacooley.com/MindShifts4Success

Claudia Cooley is on a mission to inspire others to live their most empowered life. That's exactly why she founded Claudia Cooley, Inc., a Professional Success and Life Enrichment company, where for over three decades she's provided workshops, programs and products designed to build your life and business with momentum and fulfillment. Always keeping your bottom line in mind, her focus is to expand and enrich all areas of your life: Your Health, Wealth, Relationships, Legacy, and Branding (how the world sees you). It's all about "Building Your Success Synergy."

As an accomplished Success Mentor and Mind Shift Business Coach, Claudia shares dynamic methods to empower men and women to enhance and express their unique gifts, talents, vision and dreams to bring more happiness, fulfillment, and real significance to their lives. A vibrant speaker with a slightly humorous style, Claudia draws upon her innate talents as an inspiring communicator, delivering high-energy presentations, trainings and workshops to audiences everywhere. Her clients include entrepreneurs, authors, business leaders, and individuals committed to living a life they love – one that allows them to live personal excellence and to give to others powerfully.

Claudia is the Author of *From Dud to Stud...Revving up for Success* and *Savvy Women Revving Up For Success: Women Making a Difference in the World Today*; Creator of *The 7 Mind Shifts to Ignite Your Success* Coaching System; and Host /Producer of *Rev Up For Success* Radio show.

For more information about Claudia Cooley,
visit: www.ClaudiaCooley.com